# *Children's Songs*

**by**

**Mary Rice Hopkins**

**Songs from *Big Steps for Little Feet* and *Fingerprints***

St. Paul Books & Media

The songs from this book are available on stereo cassettes, *Big Steps for Little Feet* (KC011) and *Fingerprints* (KC012).

KS011
ISBN 0-8198-1460-1

Cover design and photo by Edd Anthony, OFM, Franciscan Canticle, Inc.

Artwork by Linda Yaussi and Dan McGowan

Transcribed and engraved by Phil Perkins



Printed in the U.S.A.

## *Contents*


Big Steps . . . . 4
Little Is Much . . . . 6
Easter Rise Up . . . . 7
The Little Baby . . . . 8
Celebration Song . . . . 9
Sleep, Little One . . . . 11
It Is Good . . . . 13
A Dad Like You . . . . 14
Goobers . . . . 16
Count It All Joy . . . . 18
Everywhere . . . . 19
God's Love . . . . 20
Walk Like Jesus . . . . 22
Hip Hip Hooray . . . . 24
Gramma's House . . . . 25
Sharing Comes 'Round Again . . . . 27
Give It Away . . . . 29
My Pout Can't Come Out . . . . 30
Great Big God I Know . . . . 32
Fingerprints . . . . 34
Pray Away . . . . 36
Chicken Lips . . . . 37
Joy Is My Strength . . . . 38
If I Could Give You . . . . 39

# Big Steps

Words and Music by
Mary Rice Hopkins

E
A
My feet are small, it takes me a while.__ Some-

E
B7
E
times it seems a block is a mile.__ But lit - tle is much,

A
E
B7
E
Je - sus loves me, I've got big steps for lit-tle feet.___ I've got

Chorus
E
A
E
big steps, lit - tle feet___ I've got big steps,

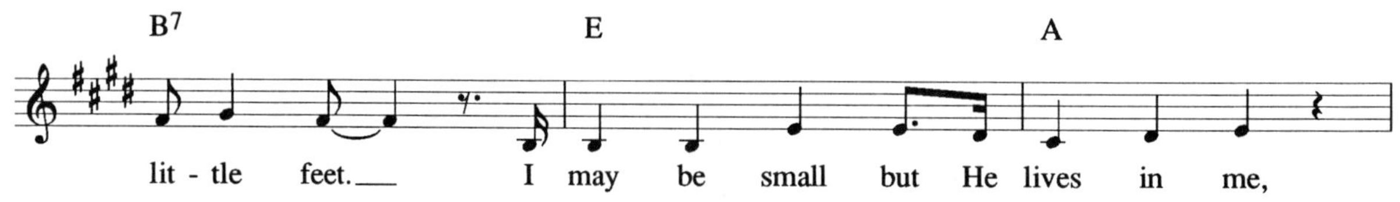
B7
E
A
lit - tle feet.___ I may be small but He lives in me,

1,2
3
E
B7
E
E
big steps, lit - tle feet.
2.My
3.In
His

A
E
A
word is a lamp,
He is a light
un - to my path
both

E
A
E
day and night.
I will not fear,
He is near.

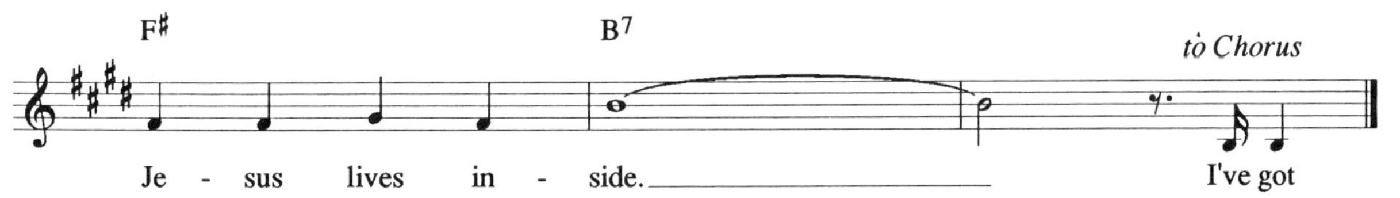
F#
B7
to Chorus
Je - sus lives in - side.
I've got

2. My God is big so look inside
He does big things in a smaller size
When I am weak, He is my strength
With each step I take. (Chorus)

3. In my heart and in these hands
I hold the future to this land.
I know where I'm going, I know who I am
I know just why I stand. (Chorus)

# Little Is Much

Words and Music by
Mary Rice Hopkins

F　　B♭　　C
**Chorus**
Lit - tle is much__ when He lives in your heart.__ Lit - tle is much__ when you

B♭/F
F
F
B♭
know who you are.__
Lit - tle is much__
when He
lives in your heart,__

C
F
Verse
F
lit - tle is much.__
1.Da - vid was a shep-herd who

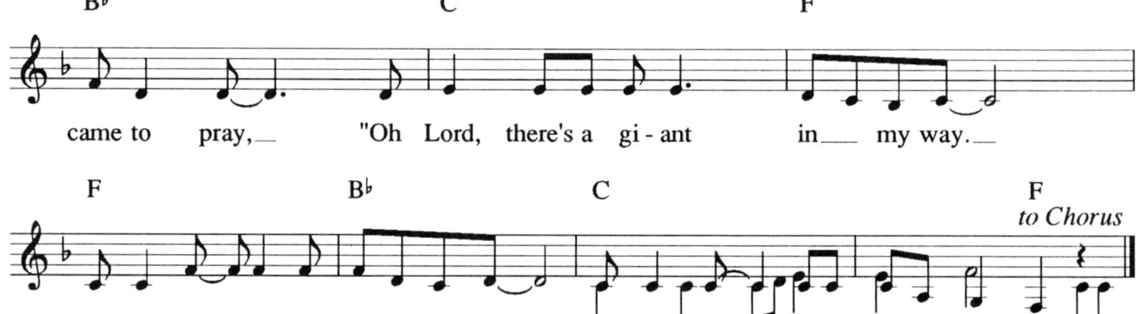
B♭
C
F
came to pray,__ "Oh Lord, there's a gi - ant in__ my way.__
F
B♭
C
F
to Chorus
With his sling - shot Go - li-ath was slain.__ Down he came__ like a gi-ant earth quake .

2. Zacheus was small, he could not see,
so he climbed up high in a tree.
Jesus said, "Come down and follow me
Hear these words that I speak. (repeat verse)
I have come for the children, I have come for you
Through my name, greater things you will do.
Whether you are a baby brand new
or if you are a hundred and two." (Chorus)

3. Moses never liked to speak
When he tried, his knees got weak.
He felt such pressure he was under the heat,
But with the words God gave him, he parted
the sea. (Chorus)

# Easter Rise Up

Words and Music by
Mary Rice Hopkins

D A D A
1.Stand up, turn a - round, touch the ground,
D A D D A
For I am a - live. I can dance, I can sing, I can
D A D A D D A
do so man-y things, and I'll tell you the rea - son why. He rose up from the
D D/F# A/E D
grave. He rose up from the grave. He
G D G A D
is not dead, He is a - live, He rose up from the grave.

2. I can run, I can walk, I can listen, I can talk
I am glad to be alive.
I can work, I can play, I am happy to say,
This is the reason why (Chorus 1)

**Chorus 2 - last time only**
Rise up, oh children, rise up, oh children
We are not dead, we are alive
Rise up, oh children

# The Little Baby

Words and Music by
Mary Rice Hopkins

E B/D♯ C♯m G♯m/B A E/G♯
Lis - ten to the sound, church bells ring - ing. Lis - ten to the sound,
F♯m7 B4 B E B/D♯ C♯m7 G♯m/B
chil - dren sing - ing. It's Christ - mas Day when Je - sus was born, the
F♯m7 E/G♯ F♯m7 B E A E/G♯
King of Kings and Lord of Lords, the King of Kings and
F♯m7 B E A E/G♯ F♯m7 E
Lord of Lords. La la la la lies the lit - tle ba - by
A E F♯m7 B E A E/G♯
la la la la Hal - le - lu - jah, la la la la lies the
F♯m7 E A E/G♯ F♯m7 B E
lit - tle ba - by la la la la Hal - le - lu - jah.

2. Wise men came from far away
To Bethlehem where He lay.
He was the Savior they had waited for
The King of Kings and Lord of Lords,
The King of Kings and Lord of Lords.
La la la la, etc.

3. Come to the manger, give your heart to Him
Give this gift that will live within.
For He gave His life and so much more
The King of Kings and Lord of Lords,
The King of Kings and Lord of Lords.
La la la la, etc.

# Celebration Song

Words and Music by
Mary Rice Hopkins

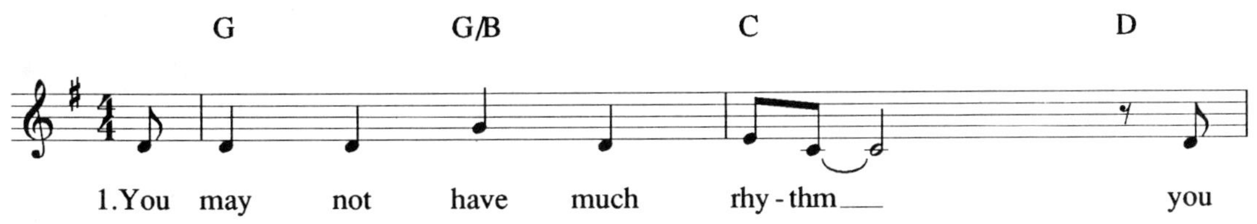
G G/B C D
1.You may not have much rhy - thm you

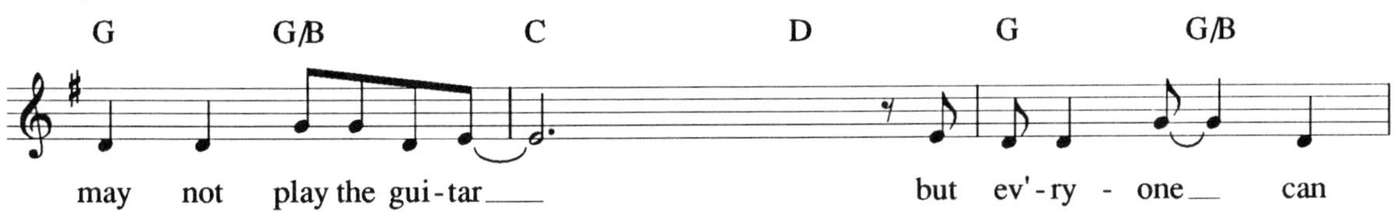
G G/B C D G G/B
may not play the gui - tar but ev' - ry - one can

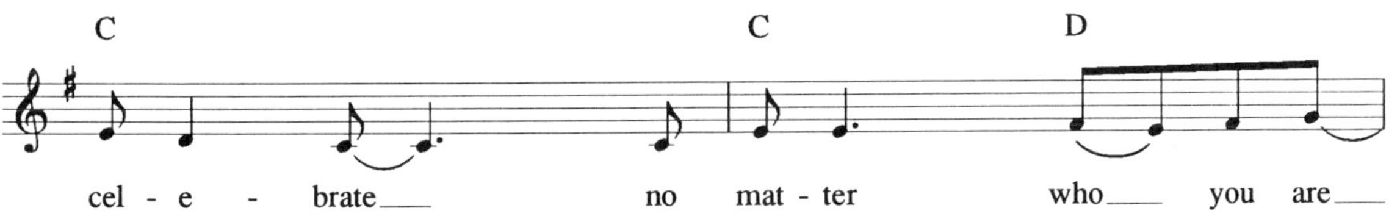
C C D
cel - e - brate no mat - ter who you are

G G G/B C D
2. If you have feet, then you can dance, If you

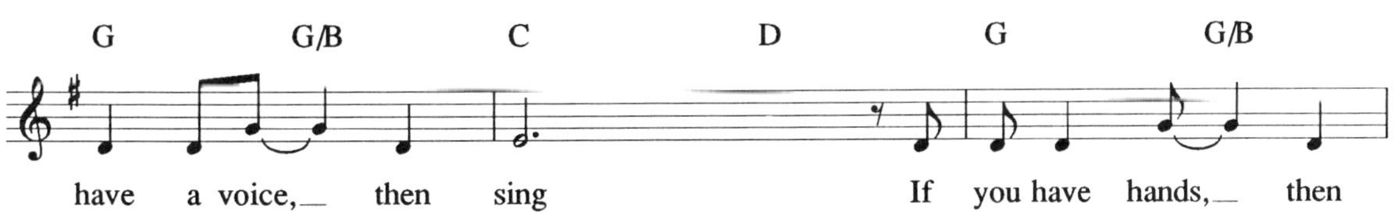
G G/B C D G G/B
have a voice, then sing If you have hands, then

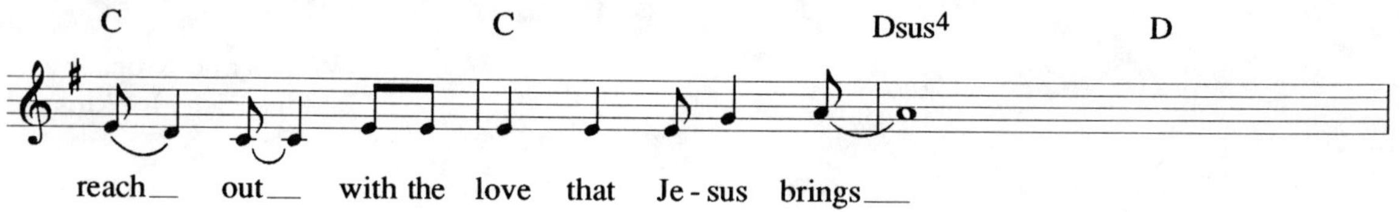
C
C
Dsus4
D
reach_ out_ with the love that Je - sus brings_

Dsus4
D
C
Chorus
D
G
G/B
So c'-mon, sing_ a-long_

C
D
G
G/B
C
D
shake some - bo - dy's hand._ Let's cel - e - brate_ what

G
G/B
C
D
G
God has done_ with His fam - i - ly_ of friends._ 3. (You)

3. You may not play the violin
You may not play the harp
But everyone can celebrate
No matter who you are.

4. If you have a face, then you can smile
If you have eyes that can see
Celebrating comes from inside
The hearts of you and me.

(Chorus)

5. He gave us mountains that climb so high and
He gave us trees to bring shade
He gave us God's word to look inside
The hearts of those He made.

6. He gave us friends that help us thru and
He gave us songs in the night.
He gave us clouds when the sky is not blue
He gave us the sun to bring light.

(Chorus)

# Sleep, Little One

Words and Music by
Mary Rice Hopkins

G C Dsus4 D
1. Come and rest your head a - gain to-night, As the
2. made the moon, the night, the stars a - bove, And they're
G C Dsus4 D Em
sun went down, God turned out the light. But soon the day will come a - gain, the
just like you the friends that you think of But you nev - er have to be a - fraid, you're
Em/D C Am7 C/D D
Chorus
sun will rise but un - til then, Dream a - bout the love in your life. Oh
not a - lone, it's O. K. He's there with His blan - ket of love.
G G/B C C/B Am D
sleep, lit - tle one. Rest a - gain un - til the morn-ing comes.
G D G G/B C C/B
Oh sleep in gen - tle peace.

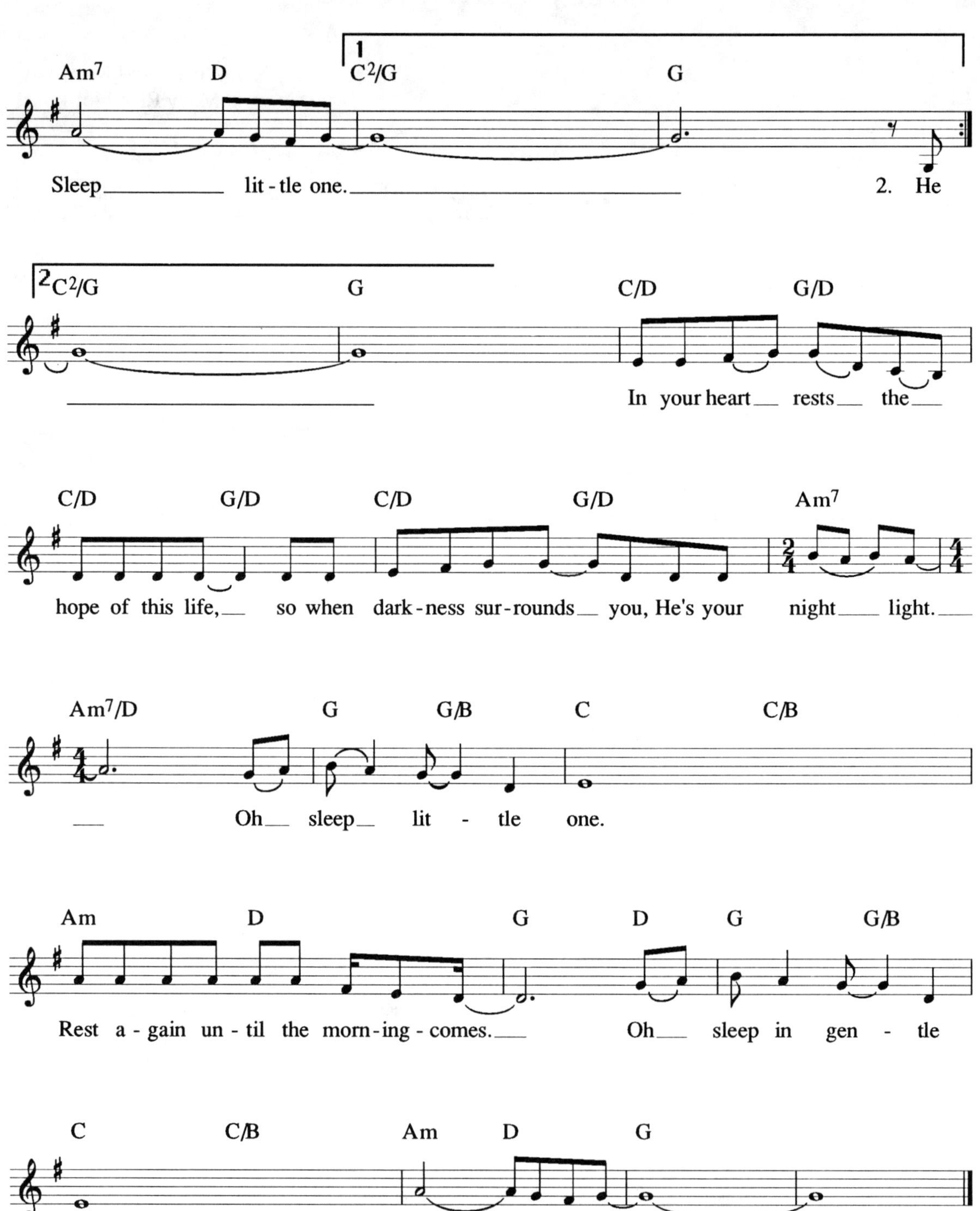

Am7 D 1 C2/G G
Sleep lit-tle one. 2. He
2 C2/G G C/D G/D
In your heart rests the
C/D G/D C/D G/D Am7
hope of this life, so when dark-ness sur-rounds you, He's your night light.
Am7/D G G/B C C/B
Oh sleep lit - tle one.
Am D G D G G/B
Rest a-gain un-til the morn-ing-comes. Oh sleep in gen - tle
C C/B Am D G
peace. Sleep lit-tle one.

# It Is Good

Words and Music by
Mary Rice Hopkins

Chorus
D A D
It is good, It is good, it is
G A D A D A
good to give thanks to the Lord. It is good, it is
D G A
good, it is good to give thanks to the
D Verses G A D G
Lord. I'll thank Him when I wake up, I'll thank Him when I lay down,
G A D G A
when I work and play. I'll thank Him 'cause He loves me,
D G A to Chorus
thank Him cause I love Him, all through - out my day.

2. I'll thank Him for my grandpa
For Mom and Dad and gramma
And those I'm not sure of
Those that I forget and I haven't met
And my best friend that I love. (Chorus)

3. I'll thank Him for my dinner,
Breakfast was a winner
Snack time in between
Thank Him for the lunch and the ladies brunch
My meat and potatoes and beans. (Chorus)

# A Dad Like You

Words and Music by
Mary Rice Hopkins/
Michael Wilke

D A E A D
La la la la la la___ la la la___ la la la___ la la la la la la___

A E A E F♯m
___ la la la___ la la la

**Verse**

1. You were there___ to___ pick me up___ when I

D E A A E
skinned my knees___ a - gain.___ It went a - way___ when you said,

F♯m Bm7 E A
"it's o - kay."___ I'm so glad___ we're friends.

**Chorus**

So

E F♯m D D A
man - y can be___ a fa - ther___ but not just an - y one can be a dad.___

E A E F♯m D
___ It takes some - one like you___ to love___ me like you do. It

Bm7 C#m D E 1 A D
takes a dad - dy, it takes a dad, like you. La la la la la la
A E A D A E
la la la la la la La la la la la la la la la la la la
2 A Last time Fine D A E A
you. There's on - ly one heav - en - ly Fa - ther. Who
D A E A D E
al - ways walks and talks with me. And He's al - ways there
C#m F#m Bm C#m D E
in my heart. He will ne - ver leave, He's hold - ing
A D A E A D A E to Verse 3
me. La la la la la la la la la la la la la la la la la la la la la la la la

2. You listened to me when I went on and on
You only feel asleep one time
If I could choose, I would pick you
I'm so glad you're mine.
(Chorus)

3. You kept me safe when what I did was wrong
You showed me the right way.
With all that we've done, I see how far I've come
And I thank you for yesterday.
(Chorus)

# Goobers

Words and Music by
Mary Rice Hopkins

C♯m
F♯m
Lurk - ing in the back - ground creep - ing all a - round, There's
B
C♯m
one who can turn a smile_ to a frown. Don't let the goo - bers
F♯m
B
C♯m
come and get you down, think a - bout the good that you've found.
E
B
Like ice cream sun - daes, trips to the zoo, and
(D. S.) Live what is right and what is true. Good
C♯m
G♯m
days that are sun - ny, a friend that's true,
things will come ________ when you do, but
A
E
1 A
B
rid - ing a horse and sing - ing too, but don't let the goo - bers get to
if it comes back when you're feel - in' blue

2,3
C♯m
A
B
you.
2. They don't let the goo-bers get to
C♯m
A
B
you,
don't let the goo-bers get to
C♯m
last time
Fine
you.
3. So
C♯m
B
when you're af-raid__ and can't be__ sure of what's in - side__ or be -
C♯m
B
hind the__ door. Just lock 'em in the base - ment un-der the__ floor and
C♯m
D. S. al Fine
think up - on__ the Lord.

2. They may be watching when you hurt inside
Or try to trip you and you can not hide
You may not be ready for their disguise
So don't let the goobers in your life. (Chorus)

# Count It All Joy

Words and Music by
Mary Rice Hopkins

Chorus
E B E A
A one and a two and a three and a four,
E B E E B
Count it all joy 'cause you know the Lord. A one and a two and a
E A E B E
Fine
three and a four, Count it all joy 'cause you know the Lord.
Verse
A E A B
1.Count my fin - gers, count my toes, but I've on - ly got one
D B E A E
mouth, one nose. Count my joy and bless - ings too, His
A Bsus B
good - ness is for me and you.
A

2. Each hair is numbered on my head
The times I rise and go to bed
How many hours I walk and stand
Oh Lord count me in. (Chorus)

# Everywhere

Words and Music by
Mary Rice Hopkins

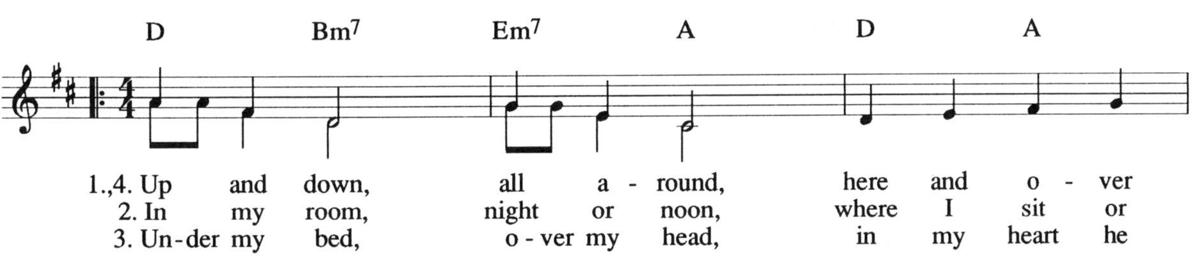
D
Bm7
Em7
A
D
A
1.,4. Up and down, all a - round, here and o - ver
2. In my room, night or noon, where I sit or
3. Un-der my bed, o - ver my head, in my heart he

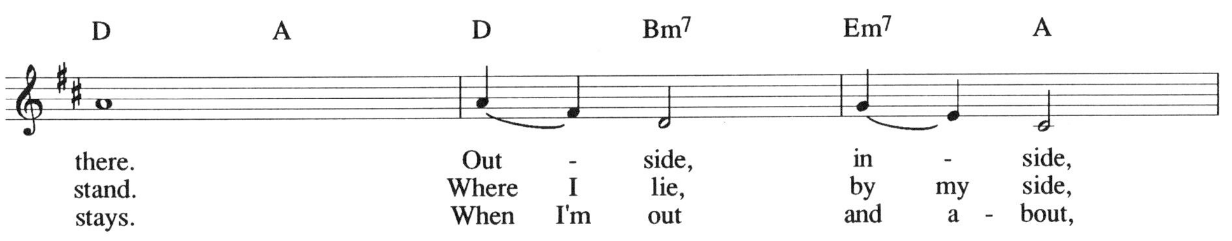
D
A
D
Bm7
Em7
A
there. Out - side, in - side,
stand. Where I lie, by my side,
stays. When I'm out and a - bout,

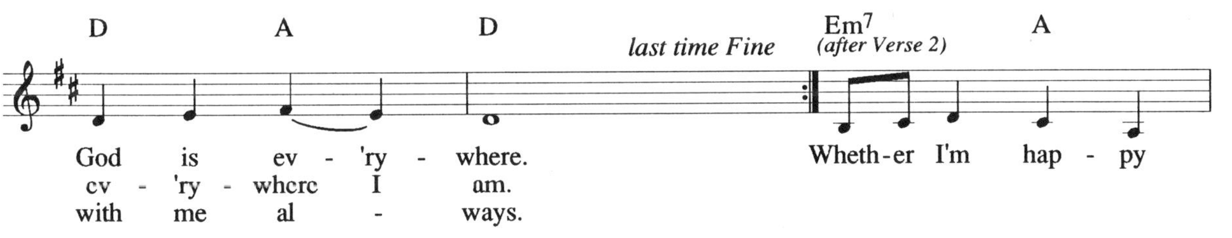
D
A
D
last time Fine
Em7
(after Verse 2)
A
God is ev - 'ry - where. Wheth-er I'm hap - py
ev - 'ry - where I am.
with me al - ways.

Em7
A
Em7
A
Em7
A
D. C. al Fine
or if I'm sad, He's with me when good or bad.

# God's Love

Words and Music by
Mary Rice Hopkins

E B/D♯ C♯m B
1.Love is go - ing the ex - tra mile when you
A B E E B/D♯
don't feel like go-ing a block. Love is giv - ing
C♯m B A B
your last dime when a dime is all you've got.
E B/D♯ C♯m B A B
Love is be-ing kind to your neigh - bor when he is-n't kind to
E E B/D♯ C♯m B
you. Love is do-ing Mom a fa - vor
A B E A B
just 'cause she asked you to.
Chorus
God's love is

G♯m
C♯m
F♯m
B
pa - tient,
God's
love is true.
E
A
B
G♯m
C♯m
God's love will bring out the
A
B
E
last time
Fine
Repeat 1 time
best in me and you.
B
E
B
Love will love no mat - ter when,
love is love un -
E
B
E
til the end.
I love you
just be - cause
F♯
B
to Chorus
God gave me a heart of love.

2. Lovc is walking with someone when they need a helping hand
Love is being true to them when they need a faithful friend
Love is loving even when it's the hardest thing to do
Love is love when it comes from inside of me and you. (Chorus)

# Walk Like Jesus

Words and Music by
Mary Rice Hopkins

Lively
1st Chorus
A D A
I want to walk, walk like Je - sus.
A E A A
I want to go where - ev - er - He goes. I want to walk,
D A A E
last time to CODA
walk like Je - sus, for I know He loves me so.
A D A
Verse
1. If I walk in
E A D A E
Je - sus' love. I will share His love with you. I'll
D A E7 A D A
be your friend ev - en when love is hard to do.
E E7 A
Repeat 2x
2nd Chorus
I want to fol - low,

D A A E A
fol - low the lead - er. I want to go where - ev - er He goes.
A D A A
I want to fol - low, fol - low the lead - er. For I know He
E A A D A
loves me so. I'll be His voice, I'll be His feet, I'll
A E A
be His hands to ev - 'ry one I meet. A - walk - in' and talk - in' and
D A A E A
(to 1st Chorus)
lov - in' like Him. I'll be His feet where - ev - er I am.
Coda
E A A
loves me so. For I know He
E A A E7 A
loves me so. For the Bi - ble tells me so.

2. Walk by faith and not by sight,
For our eyes can't always see.
He is a lamp unto my feet
In God, I can believe. (to Verse 3)

3. We need to walk hand in hand
Helping those in need.
Many come but He makes us all one
We are God's family. (to 2nd Chorus)

# Hip Hip Hooray

Words and Music by
Mary Rice Hopkins

E♭
A♭
E♭
1. In the be-gin - ning, God made the sea and the for - est

B♭
E♭
A♭
E♭
filled with trees, He made the moun - tains up so high, on the

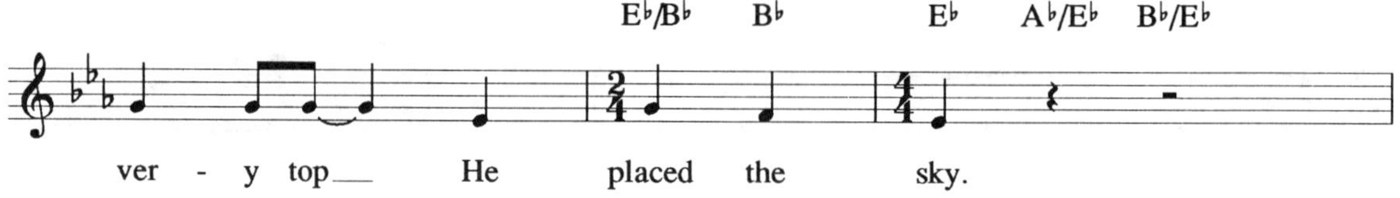
E♭/B♭
B♭
E♭
A♭/E♭
B♭/E♭
ver - y top He placed the sky.

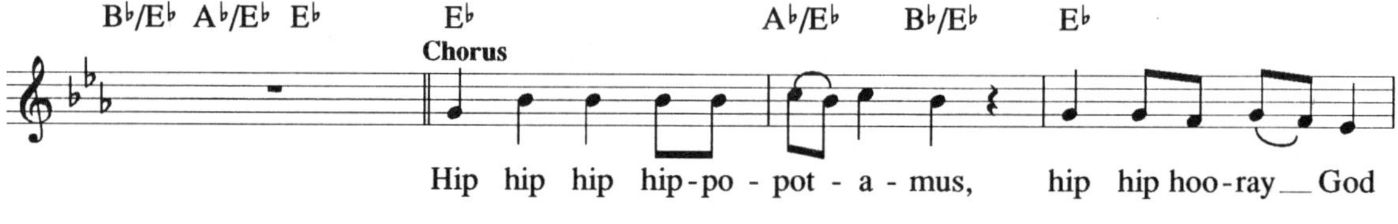
B♭/E♭
A♭/E♭
E♭
E♭
Chorus
A♭/E♭
B♭/E♭
E♭
Hip hip hip hip-po - pot - a - mus, hip hip hoo-ray God

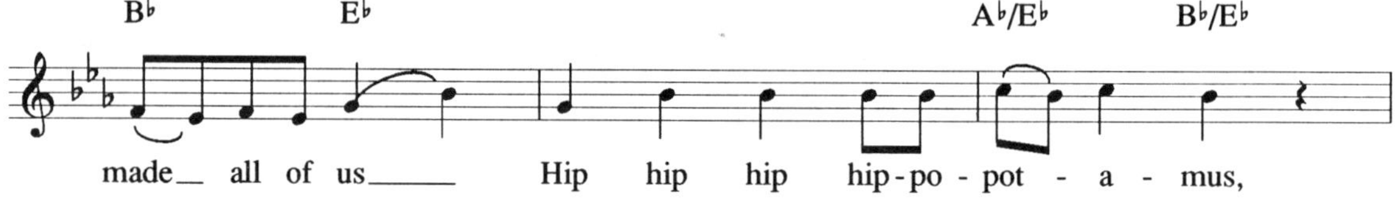
B♭
E♭
A♭/E♭
B♭/E♭
made all of us Hip hip hip hip-po - pot - a - mus,

E♭
B♭
E♭
hip hip hoo-ray He made us.

2. God's Fingerprints are everywhere
Just to show how much He cares
But in between He had loads of fun
He made a hippo who weighs a ton.
(Chorus)

3. God made the ground to stand upon
To hold the water in the ponds
Many kinds, He made everyone
But some things He just made for fun.
(Chorus)

4. Creation sings of His praise
The sparrow and the tiny babe
We can sing and say well done
But some things he just made for fun.
(Chorus)

# Gramma's House

Words and Music by
Mary Rice Hopkins

B♭ F/A B♭ F/A
1.My teach-ers give me les-sons I need to do. My
B♭ Gm Cm7 F7
par-ents give me chores and say they're good for you. My
E♭ F Dm Gm Cm7
friends are nice but they give me ad-vice but there's one place I can kick off my shoes.
Fsus7 F B♭ Gm Cm7 F7
Chorus
At Gram-ma's house, at Gram-ma's house,
B♭ F/A B♭ F/A B♭ Gm
I'm al-ways wel-come with-out a doubt. No chores to do and good-ies
Cm7 F7 B♭ Cm7 F7 1 B♭
I can't re-fuse, so wel-come to Gram-ma's house. 2. She

2.
B♭ E♭ E♭/D
house. There are lots of gram - ma's and
Cm7 F7 B♭ B♭/A Gm Gm/F
gram-pa's too,__ look-in' for a grand-kid like me and you.__ A -
E♭ E♭/D Cm7 F7 Cm7
dopt your-self one__ no-bod-y has to be blue.__ There's so much we can do.__
F7 B♭ Gm Cm7 F7
__ At Gram-ma's house,__ at Gram - ma's house,
B♭ F/A B♭ F/A B♭ Gm
I'm al-ways wel - come with-out a doubt__ no chores to do__ and good-ies
Cm7 F7 B♭ Cm7 F7 B♭
I can't re - fuse,__ so wel-come to gram - ma's house.

2. She makes me custard that just can't be beat.
She never gets mad though there's mud on my feet.
She laughts at my jokes, I sure like my grand folks,
And I just can't wait to be. (Chorus)

# Sharing Comes 'Round Again

Words and Music by
Mary Rice Hopkins/
Denny Bouchard

E A B7
1. So man - y say, "gim - me, gim - me, gim - me, gim - me," but
E A7 B7 E
I say "Share, share, share a - gain." So man - y say, "Gim - me, gim -
A B7 E A
- me, gim - me, gim - me." I wan - na share, I wan - na share with them.
B7 A B7
Chorus
Share with your neigh - bors, share
E/G♯ A B7 E
with your friends, Give of your - self, shar - ing be - gins
A B7 E/G♯ A
Let's take turns, ev - 'ry bod - y wins.
A E A E
When I start to do my part,
A B7 1 E A E
shar - ing comes 'round a - gain. A - round and a - round and a

A E A B7 E
round and a - round, shar - ing comes 'round a - gain. 2. So
2 E Amaj7 B6
If I had a loaf of bread I'd
E A F♯m7
share half with you. There'd be some for
B F♯7/A♯ B7
both of us, for I'd be shar - ing it too.
A B7 E A A B7
Share with your neigh - bors, share with your friends. Give of your - self,
E A B7 E
shar - ing be - gins Let's take turns ev - 'ry bod - y
A A E
wins. When I start to
A E A B7 E
do my part, shar - ing comes round a - gain.

2. So many say, "gimme, gimme, gimme, gimme,"
But if we take turns, you can have some too.
So many say, "Gimme, gimme, gimme, gimme,"
But there's some for me and there's some for you
(Chorus)

# Give It Away

Words and Music by
Mary Rice Hopkins

Swing
E
C♯m
1.If you've got a lit - tle love, give it a - way,
F♯m B7 E E
hey, hey, hey, If you've got a lit - tle love,
C♯m F♯m B7 A
give it a - way, hey, hey, hey. Let your love keep
E G♯7 C♯m
shin - ing through in all you say and all you do. If you've
E C♯m F♯m7 B7 E
got a lit - tle love, give it a - way, hey, hey, hey. 2. If you've

2. If you've got a little light, give it away, hey, hey, hey
   If you've got a little light, give it away, hey, hey, hey
   Let your light keep shining bright, All day long and thru the night.
   If you've got a little light, give it away, hey, hey, hey

3. If you've got a little joy, give it away, hey, hey, hey
   If you've got a little joy, give it away, hey, hey, hey
   Pass it around and spread your joy, to every girl and every boy.
   If you've got a little joy, give it away, hey, hey, hey.

4. If you've got a little peace, give it away, hey, hey, hey
   If you've got a little peace, give it away, hey, hey, hey
   We need peace and quiet times, to still all that is on our minds.
   If you've got a little peace,give it away, hey, hey, hey

# My Pout Can't Come Out

Words and Music by
Mary Rice Hopkins

E B7 E
1.I can be sweet as hon - ey, or
A B E B7
so - ur like a pic - kle to you. I can smile and be
E A B
fun - ny, or frown down to my shoes.
A B E
It's so ea - sy to pout but that's
A B E A B
not what life's a-bout. 'Cause if I get too
G#m C#m F#m B7 E
se - ri-ous my smile just won't come out.

Chorus

A
B7
E
A
B7
I can gig - gle and wig - gle or I can be such a so - ur

E
A
B7
E
pic - kle. I can be sweet as hon - ey, and

A
B7
E
A
E
laugh when things are fun - ny. But my pout just can't come

A
E
A
B
E
out to - day,___ No it can't come out to play.___ No my

A
E
A
E
A
B
E
pout just can't come out to - day___ No it can't come out to play.___

2. Nobody likes somebody who always likes to frown
We need to change the pouters, gotta turn them upside down.
'Cause when they start to smile, people follow them,
But when they pout without a doubt, they've got a lot less friends.
(Chorus)

# Great Big God I Know

Words and Music by
Mary Rice Hopkins

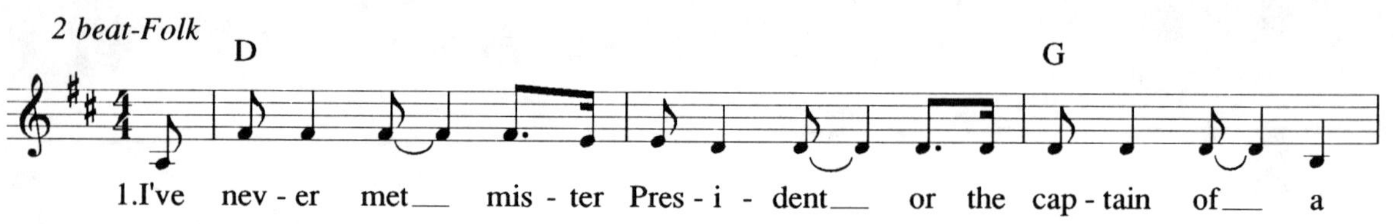
2 beat-Folk
D
G
1.I've nev - er met mis - ter Pres - i - dent or the cap - tain of a

D
D
ship. I don't know an - y mov - ie stars,

A7
G
ev - en a lit - tle bit. I'm not im - pressed by

A7
D
D/C♯
Bm
G
Ram - bo or the migh - ty Her - cu - les, but I know the King of

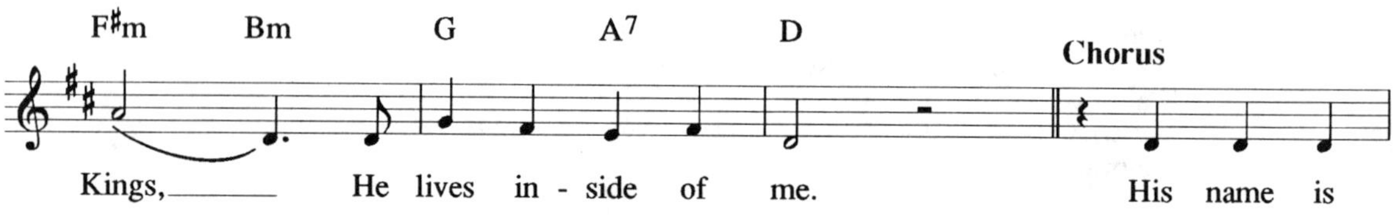
F♯m
Bm
G
A7
D
Chorus
Kings, He lives in - side of me. His name is

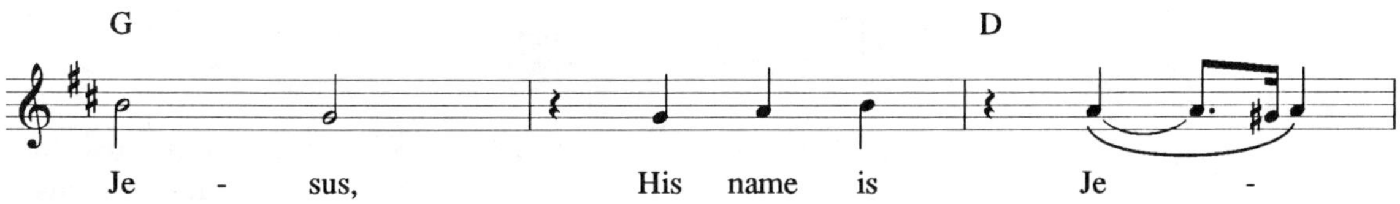
G
D
Je - sus, His name is Je -

Bm
A7
sus. The great - est one I know,__ He's

D
D7
G
with me where I go.__ His name is Je - sus

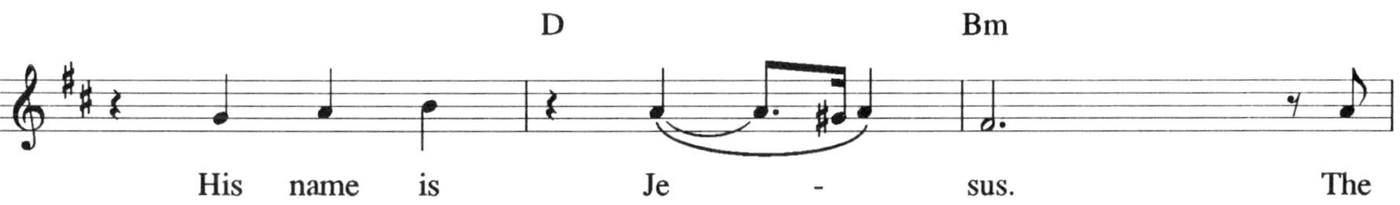
D
Bm
His name is Je - sus. The

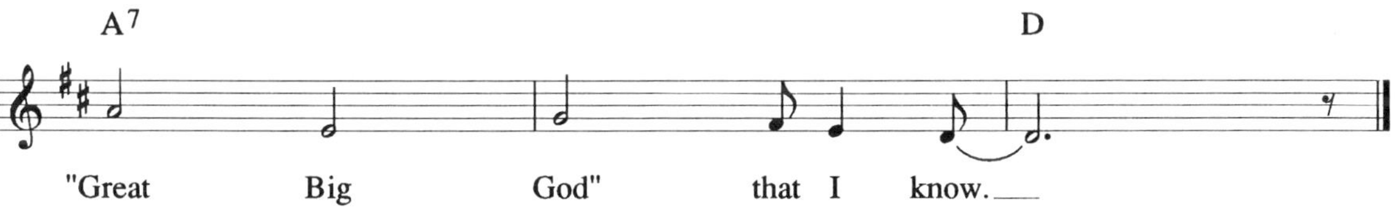
A7
D
"Great Big God" that I know.__

2. I've never seen Superman flyin' through the air
I wouldn't call Ghostbusters if a ghost appeared.
Well there's a lot thats make believe like on the TV screen,
But there is one who is for real, He is the King of Kings.
(Chorus)

3. The men of the Bible were mighty and so brave
Like Daniel in the lion's den, Oh, he was not afraid.
He stood up for his God, like Peter, James and John
He stood up for the greatest name, now he lives on and on.
(Chorus)

# Fingerprints

Words and Music by
Mary Rice Hopkins

G
C
1.When you find___ my lit - tle fin - ger - prints___ all

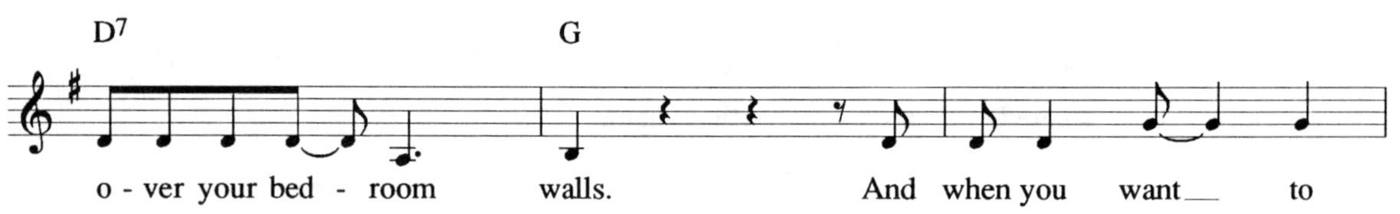
D7
G
o - ver your bed - room walls. And when you want___ to

C
D7
G
Chorus
yell a bit___ cause they're e - ven in___ the halls. I

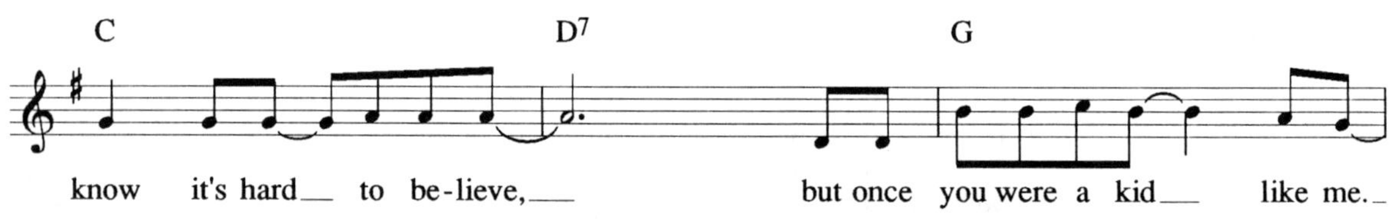
C
D7
G
know it's hard___ to be-lieve,___ but once you were a kid___ like me._

C
Am7
D7
One day I'm___ gon-na grow_____ up,___ so re -

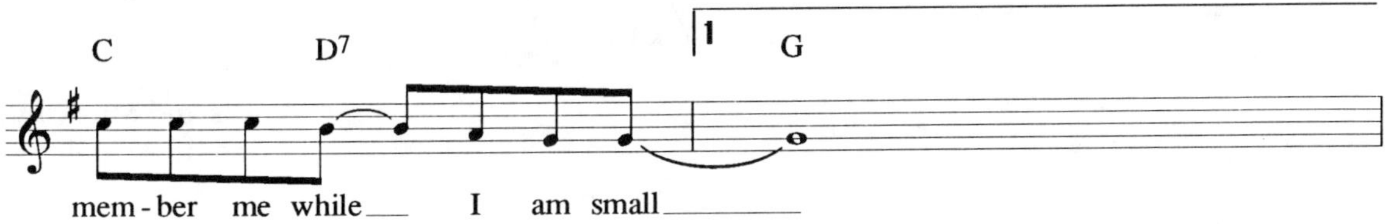
C
D7
1
G
mem - ber me while I am small

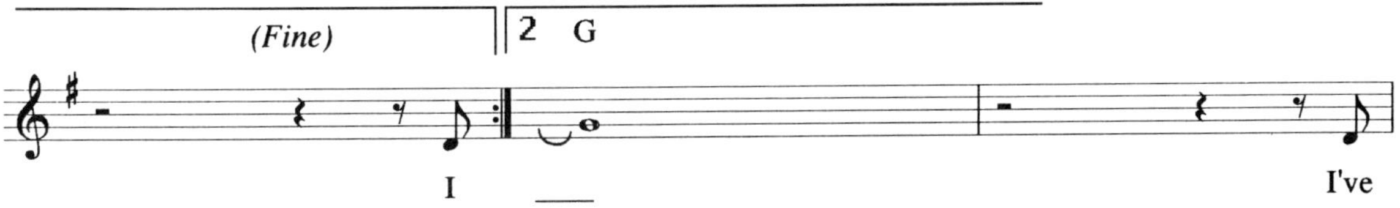
(Fine)
2 G
I
I've

C
G/B
D7
heard that where your trea - sure is, that's where your heart will

G
C
G
be. I don't know much a - bout hearts and things, but I'm

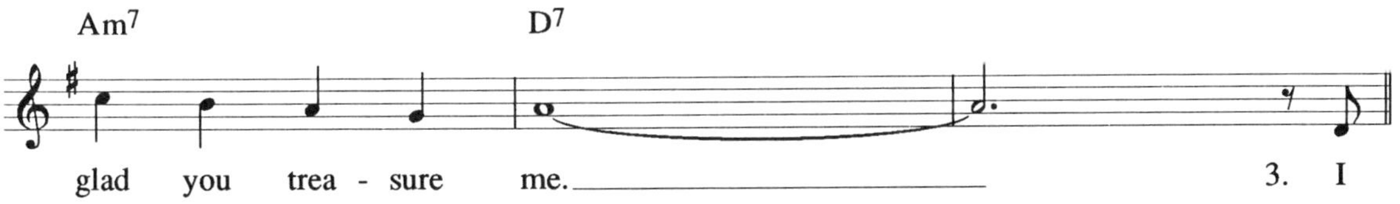
Am7
D7
glad you trea - sure me.
3. I

2. I get in the way a lot of the time
Though I'm only three feet tall.
I make you forget what's on your mind
You trip over my toys and fall. (Chorus)

3. I wanna make great fingerprints,
But I promise not on your walls.
I wanna touch those around me,
Though I'm only three feet tall. (Chorus)

# Pray Away

Words and Music by
Mary Rice Hopkins

Chorus
I'm gon - na pray a - way an - y - thing that scares me to - night and it - 'll be al - right.
I'm gon - na pray a - way ev - 'ry - thing, I won't be a - fraid of the night.
I'll pray them a - way ev - 'ry night.
1.When the lights are out, things are stir - rin' a - bout, when I feel a - lone, and I start to doubt, I pray a - way the wrong and I sing this song, and the mon - sters they're all gone.
to Chorus

2. All those scary things you might have heard of them,
   Oh they come to haunt me again and again.
   They may be under my bed or just in my head,
   But I've learned to pray instead.

# Chicken Lips

Words and Music by
Mary Rice Hopkins

*Calypso*

C Dm7 G C
Chick-en lips__ or el - e - phant feet, go - ril - la arms__ or

Dm7 G7 C Dm7
rab - bit teeth,__ well ev - 'ry bod - y has a fun - ny thing or two,__ so

G7 C G7
don't wor - ry if you do.___ Don't wor - ry, wor - ry if you__ do.__

C Dm7 G7 Em7 Am
**Chorus**
__ If you're a kan - ga - roo__ well jump real high,__ if you're a

Dm7 G7 C Am Dm7 G7
bird on the loose,__ come on and fly,__ or a cock - a - doo - dle - do,

C Am
rise and__ shine.___ Come on and

Dm7 G7 C Dm7 G7 C
use those chick - en lips,___ you got to use those chick - en lips.___

2. Giraffe neck or pigeon toes,
Hippo ears, anteater nose,
Everybody has a funny thing or two
So don't worry if you do,
No, no worry, worry if you do.
(Chorus)

3. You might wish you had curly hair
Or less freckles 'cause they're everywhere.
It makes you special, It makes you, you
So worry, worry you shouldn't do,
No, no worry, worry you shouldn't do.
(Chorus)

# Joy Is My Strength

Words and Music by
Mary Rice Hopkins
F Bb
1.My bo - dy is jump - in' like a jel - ly bean. Oh it
C7 Bb F
wants to go, if you know what I mean. But I've
F Bb C7
heard that the joy of the Lord is my strength, so I'll jump for joy,
F Chorus Bb
run and not faint. From the tip of my head to my
C F Bb
ti - ny toes, I've got His joy where-ev - er I go. Tho'
Gm7 C7 Bb C7
I am small, one thing I know, His joy is my
F Bb C F
strength. His joy, joy, joy is my strength.

2. Some say I've got energy
But if you look, you can see
I take Him with me everyday
Nobody's gonna take my joy away. (Chorus)

# If I Could Give You

Words and Music by
Mary Rice Hopkins

Ballad
D A7 F#7 Bm
1.Pho - to - graphs, things we've saved,
G D/F# Em7 A7 D A7
mem - o - ries so man - y we've made. In so lit - tle time you've
F#7 Bm G D/F# Em7 A7
grown so fast but there's one thing I know in this world that will last. If
Chorus G A7 D G Em D/F#
I could give you an - y thing, more than a home, more than
Em7 A7 G A7
a dream, more than mem - o - ries that will fade
D G G/F# Em7 A7 G D
a - way, I give to you Je - sus to - day.

2. We could pass great knowledge to you
But every book in the world would not do,
We could give you our home, our love and our time
But the greatest and free gift is yours and is mine. (Chorus)